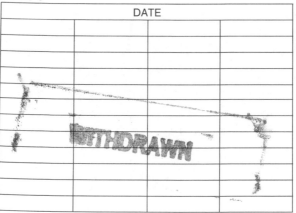

BE FIT, BE STRONG, BE YOU

by Rebecca Kajander, C.P.N.P., M.P.H.,
and Timothy Culbert, M.D.

free spirit
PUBLISHING®

Library of Congress Cataloging-in-Publication Data
Kajander, Rebecca.
  Be fit, be strong, be you / by Rebecca Kajander, and Timothy Culbert.
    p. cm.—(Be the boss of your body)
  ISBN 978-1-57542-307-4
  1. Physical fitness—Juvenile literature. 2. Diet—Juvenile literature. 3. Self-care, Health—Juvenile literature. I. Culbert, Timothy. II. Title.
  RA776.95.K35 2010
  613.7—dc22

                                                                              2009042210

At the time of this book's publication, all facts and figures cited are the most current available. All telephone numbers, addresses, and Web site URLs are accurate and active; all publications, organizations, Web sites, and other resources exist as described in this book; and all have been verified as of October 2009. The authors and Free Spirit Publishing make no warranty or guarantee concerning the information and materials given out by organizations or content found at Web sites, and we are not responsible for any changes that occur after this book's publication. If you find an error or believe that a resource listed here is not as described, please contact Free Spirit Publishing. Parents, teachers, and other adults: We strongly urge you to monitor children's use of the Internet.

The concepts, ideas, procedures, and suggestions contained in this book are not intended as substitutes for professional healthcare.

The "Get In Sync™" technique is a trademark of the Institute of HeartMath®. This technique is part of the Institute's HeartSmarts® program and has been published with their permission. Learn more about the Institute of HeartMath at www.heartmath.org.

Reading Level Grade 4; Interest Level Ages 8–13;
Fountas & Pinnell Guided Reading Level Q

Edited by Eric Braun
Illustrated by David Klug
Cover and interior design by Natasha Kenyon

10 9 8 7 6 5 4 3 2 1
Printed in Hong Kong
P17200110

Free Spirit Publishing Inc.
217 Fifth Avenue North, Suite 200
Minneapolis, MN 55401-1299
(612) 338-2068
help4kids@freespirit.com
www.freespirit.com

Dedication

To all of the children, families, colleagues, and friends who have taught us so much. —*RK and TC*

Acknowledgments

We are thankful for the professional wisdom and review of the book drafts from Joel Jahraus, M.D.; Betsy Swartz M.D.; Betty Bajwa, R.D., L.D., C.D.E.; pediatric dietitian Janie Cooperman, M.S., R.D., L.D., C.D.E.; Milagros Santiago, M.D; and Terriann Matejcek, certified yoga instructor.

We greatly appreciate Judy Galbraith and the staff at Free Spirit Publishing for recognizing the importance and timeliness of this topic and for their willingness to move forward even in challenging times. Our deepest gratitude goes to editor Eric Braun for his patience, persistence, and perfectionism in editing. His ability to put our information and ideas into kid-friendly language is amazing. The book would not be possible without the illustrator and design team for bringing our words "to life."

We acknowledge the important contributions of our professional organizations, the National Association for Pediatric Nurse Associates and Practitioners (NAPNAP) and the American Academy of Pediatrics (AAP), for their ongoing research and education in the fields of pediatric healthcare and obesity prevention.

Rebecca is grateful for the enduring friendship, wealth of information, and practical suggestions on healthy eating and exercise from Linda Morshare, B.A., M.H.A., R.N., and to her husband Jerry for his encouragement and patience.

CONTENTS

MOVIN' AND IMPROVIN': EXERCISE IS EXCELLENT 86

INTRODUCTION

Your Awesome Body

Have you ever stopped to think how awesome your body is? It's totally unique, and it's the one thing in the world that will always be all yours. It can heal wounds, kill germs, and fight infections, all on its own. Sure, sometimes you need to go to the doctor or take medicine—everybody does—but your body does an amazing job of taking care of itself . . . especially if you help it do its job.

Another reason your body is amazing is what it does with food. Imagine eating a taco. Lots of different types of **nutrients** are in tacos, like proteins, carbohydrates, fats, vitamins, and minerals. After you chew and swallow a bite, your body knows how to take it apart and turn all those good, healthy nutrients into energy. Very cool!

Food = Energy

You need energy for everything you do, like growing, running, and preventing illness—even breathing. That energy comes from food.

Your body works, feels, and looks its best when you take in about the same amount of energy as you use. That means eating the right amount of wholesome, nutritious food and getting the right amount of exercise every day. Eating a variety of foods helps make sure you get a variety of nutrients.

Taking care of yourself this way helps you feel

energized

capable

positive

motivated

attractive

sharp

strong

focused

ready for fun

ready for anything

great!

If you don't eat well or stay active enough, you may develop serious problems with your health. You also might:

★ feel sluggish, tired, or generally lousy

★ feel sad or depressed

★ have trouble concentrating

★ do poorly in school

★ feel stressed about your looks

★ not be able to keep up with friends' activities

★ feel hungry all the time

What Can You Do About Fitness and Food?

A lot, actually. You have the power to **Be the Boss of Your Body.** That means taking charge of your own health and wellness, and that's what this book is about.

Be Fit, Be Strong, Be You is filled with ideas, activities, and skills to help you

★ learn how the right food can help you be healthy

★ find the right weight for your body

★ feel better for school, sports, hobbies, and other activities

★ increase your self-confidence

★ look your best

★ discover fun ways to be active

Look for **B³ Skills** in every chapter that you can use to help yourself be healthier now and for the rest of your life. (B³ is short for **Be** the **Boss** of Your **Body**.)

Healthy, Happy You

Being fit is about more than being skinny or having big muscles.
You can be skinny and not be healthy. Being large doesn't
automatically mean you're *not* healthy. Being truly fit is about
being the *right* weight for your height and body build. People
come in many different sizes and shapes, and your body type will
likely be different from those of your friends. **And that's okay.**

Being fit also means using food to keep you healthy and
happy. It means being active. It means being confident in who
you are. And it's knowing that the way you feel about yourself
affects your health.

We wrote this book to help you do all those things, whether you feel great most of the time or would like some help feeling better. Whether you're just the right weight, overweight, or underweight. Whether you're happy with your body or wish you were happier. No matter how fit you are now, you can do more to help yourself and be in charge of your health. With the right attitude, you can be fit, be strong, and **be you.**

Are You Ready?

There is one secret to being the boss of your body.
You can succeed only if you make the choice to do it for
yourself—and not because your mom, dad, doctor, school nurse,
big brother, pet dog, best friend Harry, or anyone else wants you
to. Your motivation is power. That doesn't mean you don't need
coaching, love, support, and advice from family, friends, healthcare
providers, or teachers. It just means you have to do this for you.

Take this quiz to see how ready you are. Answer each statement
with a **1** (never), **2** (sometimes), or **3** (often). Write your answers
on a piece of paper.

1. **I skip breakfast.**

2. **I eat at fast-food restaurants.**

3. **I drink more than one can of soda a day.**

4. **I eat when I'm bored.**

5. **I eat sugar-heavy snacks like candy and ice cream.**

6. **I eat alone.**

7. **I eat while I watch TV or play video games.**

8. **I spend more than two hours a day looking at screens (TV,
   computer, video games, etc.).**

Take a look at the questions you answered with a 2 or 3. Can
you think of ways to improve in these areas? Are you ready to try?
These are important first steps to being the boss of your body.
Give yourself small goals that you can get excited about and reach.
Even if you've never thought about your fitness before, you're
reading this book—that's something! You're on your way.

We'd love to hear how the ideas in this book work for you. If you want to share your story or ask us a question, you can email us at **help4kids@freespirit.com** or send us a letter at:

Rebecca Kajander and Tim Culbert
Free Spirit Publishing
217 Fifth Avenue North, Suite 200
Minneapolis, MN 55401-1299

BODY, MIND, AND SPIRIT
Health for the Whole Self

If you eat well, get exercise, and don't get sick, you are probably pretty healthy. But did you know that good health is not only about your body? It's also about having a healthy, positive mind and spirit. Your body, mind, and spirit are connected and work together.

Your body is the physical part of yourself—all of your bones, muscles, organs, and everything else about you that takes up space in the world.

Your mind is the part of you that thinks, understands, remembers, imagines, and feels emotions. When you picture an image in your head or try to figure out a problem, you're using your mind.

Your spirit gives you feelings of hope, comfort, and peace. Your spirit connects you to things outside yourself and gives life meaning. For many people, a healthy spirit has to do with a belief in God or a higher power. A healthy spirit can also come from a feeling of connection with music, art, or nature.

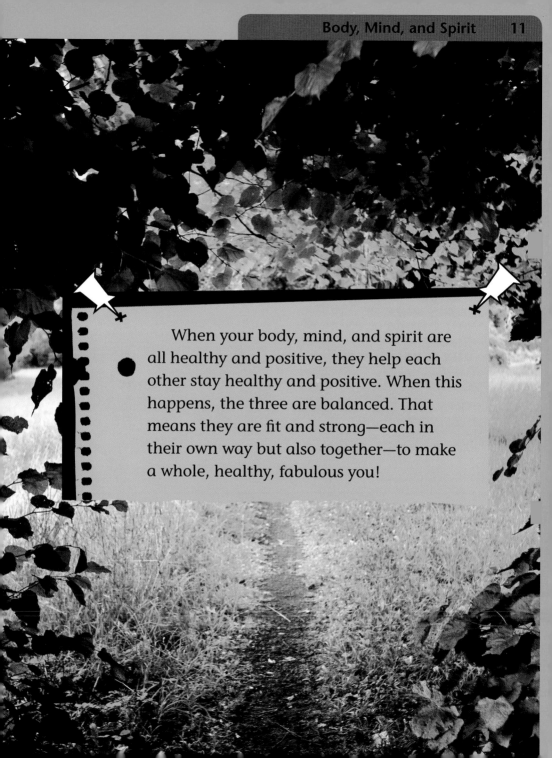

When your body, mind, and spirit are all healthy and positive, they help each other stay healthy and positive. When this happens, the three are balanced. That means they are fit and strong—each in their own way but also together—to make a whole, healthy, fabulous you!

What Does It Feel Like to Be Balanced?

Your body

* you have warm fingers and toes
* your breathing and heartbeat are regular
* your hands are dry
* your muscles are relaxed
* you have enough energy to get things done every day

Your mind

* **you have positive thoughts and emotions**

* **you feel confident, loved, grateful, proud, and safe**

* **you feel organized and able to focus attention**

Your spirit

* **you notice and appreciate beauty**
* **you feel connected to and loved by others**
* **you have a sense of peacefulness**
* **you enjoy nature**
* **you may feel some identification with God or a higher power**
* **you may engage in regular practice of meditation or prayer**

When you do things to take care of your body, mind, *and* spirit, you are healthier and feel better. And when you're healthier and feel better, you're more likely to do things that are good for your body, mind, and spirit. It's a great cycle to get into. And you know what? Healthy kids are more likely to be healthy adults, so what you learn now can help you for your whole life.

Check out the B³ skills on the following pages you can use to help strengthen the health of your whole self.

B³ skill: Belly Breathing

Belly breathing is a way of controlling your breathing in order to feel better. It relaxes your muscles, calms your nerves, and helps clear your mind. It also helps release chemicals (called endorphins) in your body that make you feel good.

Here's how you do it:

1. Get comfortable. You can be standing, sitting, or lying down.

2. Imagine you have a balloon in your belly.

3. Put your hand on top of your belly.

4. Breathe in slowly through your nose, counting to three and feeling the balloon fill with air.

5. Breathe out slowly through your mouth, counting to five and feeling the balloon get flat. Imagine that your tension and negative thoughts go out of your body as you breathe out.

6. Notice how your muscles relax as you breathe out. Imagine a picture of your muscles relaxing.

7. As you breathe in, say, "I am" or "I can be," and as you breath out, say, "healthy" or another positive idea you choose.

B³ Skill:
Get in Sync

Your heart is connected to all parts of your body. Your heartbeat responds to your emotions, both positive and negative. When you get scared, your heart beats fast. When you feel a strong emotion such as love, your heart pounds faster, too. Positive and upbeat emotions such as love and appreciation create a smooth heart rhythm. Negative emotions like anger, frustration, and worry can result in an irregular heart rhythm. Smooth heart rhythms can improve your thinking, boost your immune system, and relieve stress.

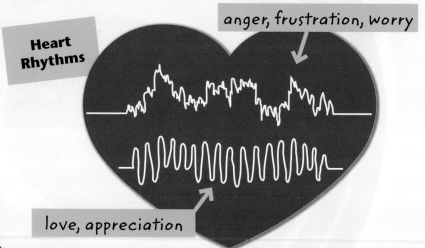

Heart Rhythms

anger, frustration, worry

love, appreciation

HeartSmarts is a program that helps people better understand and manage their heart-mind connection. With this HeartSmarts technique called Get in Sync*, you will learn how to use the power of your heart.

1. **Shift to the heart.** Focus on the area of your heart and breathe slowly and easily.

2. **Activate appreciation.** Make a sincere effort to activate a feeling of appreciation. Think of someone or something you really care about. It could be a special person in your life, a pet you love being with, or something you really enjoy doing. Build a warm feeling of sunshine in your heart. Do you feel it now? Good!

3. **Breathe the warm feeling.** Now breathe slowly and easily as you focus on the warmth in your heart. Continue doing this for one or two minutes.

If it was hard for you to find a positive feeling or attitude, take time now to think of some. Remember a couple times when you felt calm, joyous, or uplifting feelings. Write down those experiences or memorize them so they will be easy to remember when you use this HeartSmart skill.

*The "Get In Sync" technique is a trademark of the Institute of HeartMath. This technique is part of the Institute's HeartSmarts program and has been published with their permission. Learn more about the Institute of HeartMath at www.heartmath.org.

LOVE THAT PERSON IN THE MIRROR

Self-Esteem

What do you see when you look in the mirror? Do you ever think you are too tall, too short, too skinny, or too fat? Do you think your hair is too curly or too straight, or that you have too many freckles?

Those kinds of thoughts are normal for kids, and they're part of growing up. If you're going through puberty, you may have even more worries because your body is changing. You may worry that you are growing or developing too fast or too slow compared to your friends. Adjusting to these changes may be difficult, but they're normal, too.

The really important question to ask yourself is: **Who** do you see when you look in the mirror?

Do you see someone who is kind, funny, or strong? Do you see someone who is generous, smart, or athletic? Do you see a loyal friend? A dedicated student? A hard worker?

clever

honest

optimistic

upbeat

helpful

brave

trail-blazer

good listener

fun to be with

What kind of person are you?

Your Self-Image

How you see yourself is your **self-image.** If you choose to focus on positive things about yourself, your self-image will be healthier. You'll feel better about yourself, which means you have healthy **self-esteem.** Self-esteem is how you **feel** about yourself—how much confidence you have in yourself as a person. It includes how much you feel loved and valued by others, and how much you love and value yourself.

Self-image and self-esteem are important because they affect how you think and act. When you feel good about yourself, you are more likely to get along well with others. You're more likely to do well in school and enjoy being active. You can take pride in your abilities and accept your weaknesses. When you feel good about yourself, you can do your best without having to be perfect!

People who feel good about themselves are better able to handle disappointments and frustrations. They can recognize their mistakes and learn from them. And they are more likely to feel comfortable with their bodies.

Build Your Self-Esteem

You can do a lot to improve your self-image and build up your self-esteem. Start by keeping in mind that you are more than your looks. You are a one-of-a-kind person with strengths, ambitions, and ideas. Ask yourself: **what am I good at?** Maybe it's puzzles or math or writing. Maybe you're funny or you always know how to cheer up a sad friend. Maybe you always finish what you start. Maybe you make terrific omelets. Maybe your mom can always depend on you to help take care of a younger sibling. Maybe you're good at running, dancing, laughing, drawing, knitting, taking tests, doing impressions, playing cards, playing checkers, or doing Sudoku. Maybe you love stories and soak up history like a sponge, or maybe you can spell tough words like a spelling champ. Maybe you *are* a spelling champ. Maybe you know everything there is to know about dinosaurs and you just know you're going to grow up to be a paleontologist.

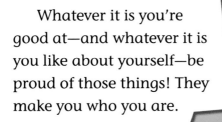

Whatever it is you're good at—and whatever it is you like about yourself—be proud of those things! They make you who you are.

Think of three things about yourself that make you special or different from everyone else, and write them down. Then keep your list and refer to it whenever you feel down about yourself. Hey, maybe you can think of *more* than three. After all: **you're awesome!**

Other ways you can improve your self-image and self-esteem:

★ ***Eat right and get enough exercise.*** You'll feel better and look better. Reading this book can help you with your food and fitness decisions.

★ ***Get enough sleep.*** Most kids between the ages of 8 and 14 need 8–10 hours a night.

★ ***Make time for fun.*** You have school, homework, sports, and other activities—and those are important. But you need to relax and have fun, too. Hang out with friends, watch a movie, play in the park, read a book, have a tickle fight with your sister, play a board game or video game . . . whatever it is that you enjoy. Make time for you.

★ ***Set reasonable standards for yourself.*** Don't expect to be perfect at the things you do, because there's no such thing. And don't be too hard on yourself when things don't go your way. Life is full of mistakes and failures. They mean you're learning, which is good.

We All Come in Different Shapes and Sizes

It can be hard to maintain high self-esteem when we see so many media images of celebrities who are considered super-attractive, totally wow-looking, or "perfect." Don't compare yourself to models, actors, and others in the media. Most of us don't look like the people who appear on TV, on the Web, and in magazines. Those people are hired specifically *because their looks are unusual.* They are often very tall or overly thin. Many times pictures of them are changed by computers to make them look even more unusual!

People are born into all different kinds of bodies, and many things influence what kind of body you have. Here are a few of them:

★ **Genetics.** *Genetics* means your *genes*—qualities built into your body. You inherit certain traits from your parents. Look at pictures of your parents, grandparents, and aunts and uncles to see if you notice physical features you have in common. Examples might be eye color, face shape, or how tall you are. Maybe a lot of people in your family get bunions on their toes. Maybe they have beautiful skin.

★ **Race and culture.** People from different parts of the world may have different skin color, hair types, and other physical features. They may carry their fat and muscle in different places on their bodies. They may also tend to be taller or shorter.

★ **Family habits.** Families teach their kids how to eat. If a family eats lots of fruits and vegetables, keeps portions smaller, and sits together for meals, those good habits can affect a kid's body—in a good way. Kids learn less-healthy eating habits in families that eat a lot of high-fat foods (like chips, cheeseburgers, and ice cream), drink lots of soda, snack often, or eat large portions at mealtime. That can affect a kid's body, too. So can the amount of activity your family gets together.

If you want to know if you are a healthy weight for your height and body shape, ask your doctor or another healthcare provider for help. He or she can also help you figure out your **body mass index (BMI).** That's a way to estimate if your height and weight are in good proportion. After you know your BMI, you can compare it to a chart that shows a healthy range of BMI for your age, sex, height, and weight.

No matter what your body type, everyone needs to have some body fat. Fat protects joints and organs, regulates body temperature, and stores vitamins. Too little body fat can put you at risk for medical problems.

A healthcare provider can also help you by asking about your diet, your physical activity, and your family history. All these things help determine how healthy you are.

B³ Skill:
★Affirmations★

Self-talk is how we talk to ourselves while doing things. By talking to yourself in a positive way, you can improve your self-image and better manage difficult situations. Scientific studies have shown that your thoughts affect how you feel.

Here's how you do it:

Talk to yourself—out loud or just in your mind—in positive, encouraging ways.

When you say something positive about yourself, it's called an "affirmation." What affirmations can you say about yourself? If you have negative thoughts about yourself, how can you turn each one into a helpful thought?

Here's a chart to get you started.

If you think:	Try thinking:
I don't care about fitness.	I want to be healthy.
I'm too tall.	I'm one-of-a-kind.
Why bother? It's too hard.	I will be good to myself today.
I don't like vegetables.	I will eat well today.
I hate soccer.	I am making myself healthier by exercising.
Exercise is boring.	Exercising helps me feel good.

Affirmations should be sincere, or honest and realistic. Don't tell yourself that you're the best goalie in your league if that's not true. And don't make big promises you can't keep, like *I will eat five servings of vegetables every day for the rest of my life.* It's best to focus on one day at a time: *I will eat two green vegetables today.* Give yourself compliments that are true and goals that are reachable, and remind yourself of real, positive truths.

Take affirmations a step further by putting them on flashcards or taping them to your mirror, MP3 player, computer, notebook, or refrigerator. Give yourself compliments every day.

I will be good to myself today.

FANTASTIC FOOD, DUDE
Eat Right to Feel Right

Do you know what a **diet** is? People often talk about "going on a diet," usually to lose weight. They might stop eating certain kinds of foods, or cut way back on how much they eat. But that kind of diet can be unhealthy for kids. Really, your diet is simply the food you eat. Whatever you put into your body to supply you with energy, that's your diet.

WHAT DOES YOUR BODY NEED?

To maintain a healthy body, mind, and spirit, your diet should contain all of these important nutrients:

* Proteins These are the "building blocks" of the body, and they're necessary for growth and for building body structures like muscle. You can find protein in meats and dairy products such as milk and cheese. Beans like soybeans and chickpeas, and nuts and fish are also good sources of protein.

* Vitamins and minerals These help prevent sickness and keep your body running its best. Fruits and vegetables are great sources of vitamins and minerals.

* Calcium This makes your bones and teeth strong. Milk, cheese, and yogurt are good sources of calcium. So are dark green vegetables (such as spinach) and tofu.

* **Fiber** Fiber helps your digestive system work its best. Our bodies can't digest fiber, so it passes through our digestive system, pushing food through as it goes. Most fruits, vegetables, and whole grains have a lot of fiber.

* **Carbohydrates** "Carbs" give your brain and body energy. Whole grain bread, rice, oatmeal, pasta, and tortillas are all good sources of carbs.

* **Oils and fat** These give you long-term energy. You need fat to absorb certain vitamins, including vitamins A, D, E, and K. Certain fats are also needed to build healthy brain cells and hormones.

You can get the nutrients you need by eating a variety of healthy foods. However, not all foods are created equal. (You knew that was coming, right?) Whole foods are natural foods that haven't been changed, prepared, or packaged. They provide more nutrients than processed foods, which *have* been changed or prepared, usually in a factory. And whole foods don't have the unhelpful extra stuff that comes in most processed foods, like artificial dyes, preservatives, and sweeteners. Whenever possible, eat fresh, organic, locally grown food.

Word Watch
Grains: foods made from a cereal grain, including rice, corn, oats, and wheat—which you can find in bread, pasta, and breakfast cereal. *Whole grains* are grains that have not been refined—which means purified or processed. Examples of whole grains are brown rice, popcorn, and whole wheat bread. White rice, white bread, and most pasta are made from refined grains. Refined grains aren't as healthy as whole grains.

The Skinny on Fat

You may have heard people talking about "good fat" vs. "bad fat." The good fat they're talking about refers to **unsaturated fats**, which are found in vegetable oils, nuts, and fish. One reason they're good is because they help you absorb vitamins. Omega-3 fatty acid is especially important for a healthy brain.

Saturated fats and **trans fats** are considered "bad" because they raise your cholesterol levels. Cholesterol is a fatty substance that can raise your risk of heart disease if you have too much of it. Bad fats can get mucked up in your blood vessels, hardening and making it difficult for blood to flow through your body. Saturated fats usually come from animal products like cheese and meats. Trans fats are naturally found in these foods, too, but they are also in vegetable oils that have been specially treated (hydrogenated) so they are solid at room temperature—like shortening.

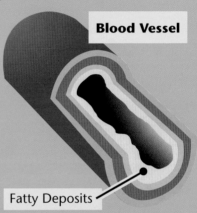

Blood Vessel

Fatty Deposits

Word Watch
Heart disease: when the heart and blood vessels don't work right. Heart disease can result in parts of the body not getting enough blood.

Mix It Up (The Colors, That Is)

An easy way to make sure you're eating the right kinds of foods is to eat a variety of colors.

★ *green:* including avocados, melons, and spinach

★ *yellow:* including bananas, peppers, and pineapples

★ *orange:* including oranges, cantaloupes, and sweet potatoes

★ *red:* including apples, grapes, peppers, and tomatoes

★ *brown:* including beans, whole wheat bread, and nuts

★ *black:* including beans, grapes, and tea

If you eat lots of different foods with a variety of colors every day, you should get plenty of nutrients. Don't be fooled by processed foods with artificial colors, like candy or those bright orange cheese curls. Look for *natural* foods that have been through little or no processing.

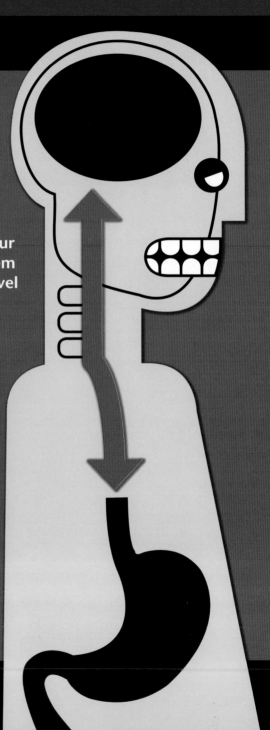

The Brain-Gut Connection

Why do we get "butterflies in our stomach" when we get nervous? Where did the saying "trust your gut" come from?

A very important connection exists between our brain and our digestive system (or the "gut"). Messages travel between the two systems all the time. For example, have you ever noticed that the thought of eating can make you feel hungry? Or that having anxious or nervous thoughts can give you a stomachache?

These messages are sent by cells called *neurons.* The lining of the gut can have as many as 100 million neurons. That's the same number as in the brain! Some experts even call the gut "the second brain." For example, the gut has more serotonin—a chemical that affects our mood and helps decrease pain—than the brain.

Because the gut is so important for brain function, it is important to keep it healthy. And guess what? That happens when we eat well and take good care of ourselves. One thing that really helps is **bacteria**.

Eew, gross! Are we supposed to eat bacteria?

Actually, yes. And you probably already do. Most of the time we think of bacteria as being bad or acting like a germ that causes illness. But actually, your gut has billions of good bacteria that help you digest and absorb the food you eat. It also has some unhealthy bacteria that can make you sick. This unhealthy bacteria may "act up" when you have an imbalance in your digestive system. To keep the right balance, you can build up the good bacteria by eating foods like yogurt and kefir. You can also take a supplement called a "probiotic," which can be helpful.

Check Out MyPyramid

The U.S. government has created a Web site called MyPyramid to help people make smarter food and fitness decisions. Go to www.MyPyramid.gov and click on "Inside the Pyramid" to learn all about recommended food groups and serving sizes, as well as tips to help you eat more healthy foods. Click on "My Pyramid Plan" and enter your age, sex, weight, height, and approximate level of activity to get personalized recommendations.

MyPyramid.gov
STEPS TO A HEALTHIER YOU

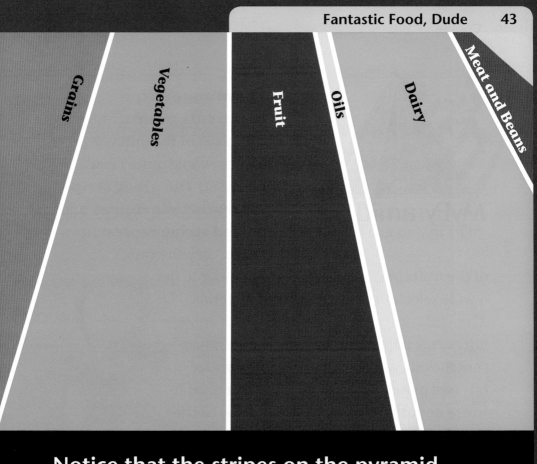

Grains

Vegetables

Fruit

Oils

Dairy

Meat and Beans

Notice that the stripes on the pyramid are not all the same width. We should eat more of the foods that have wider stripes, and less of the foods that have thinner ones.

MyPyramid.gov
STEPS TO A HEALTHIER YOU

The orange stripe represents grains. Make sure most of the grains you eat are whole grains (see page 37). **The green stripe represents vegetables** and the **red stripe represents fruit.** Vary the colors of the fruits and veggies you eat in order to get a wide selection of vitamins and minerals. **The yellow stripe is for oils,** which contain fatty acids important for your health. Make sure the oils you consume are unsaturated oils (see page 38). Most people don't need to worry about adding oils to their diets, as they get what they need from foods they already eat. You get unsaturated oils from fish, nuts, and vegetable oils used in cooking and in salad dressings.

Milk and other dairy products, such as cheese and yogurt, are represented by the blue stripe. Make most of your dairy choices fat-free or low-fat. Dairy foods are a great source of calcium, but some people are allergic to dairy. Those people can get calcium from soy, tofu, dark green veggies, and goat's milk. They can also get it from juice and cereals that are enriched with calcium.

The purple stripe is for the meat and beans group. This section is where you get most of your protein. Limit red meat to once a week. Fish, nuts, and seeds are terrific foods to fulfill your purple stripe needs, and they're better for you than red meat.

How About a Little Help Over Here!

Many kids and grown-ups take a multivitamin every day to help make sure they get all the vitamins they need. You might be thinking . . .

Great! I can eat pork rinds and cotton candy for every meal and get my nutrients from a pill. Rock on!

But hold on a second. Multivitamins do **not** replace the need to eat healthy food, because many nutrients can only come from whole foods. A multivitamin can be *helpful* for many kids, but it's not a magic health pill.

Many people take omega-3 fatty acid, too. Omega-3 fatty acids are super helpful for building a healthy brain. You can find them in fatty fish like salmon and tuna and in flaxseed and walnuts, or you can also take a supplement (a pill).

Check with your doctor or other healthcare professional if you think you should start taking an omega-3 fatty acid supplement or a multivitamin.

Walnuts

Flaxseed

Omega-3 fatty acid supplement

How Much Do You Need?

How much food your body needs depends on your age, sex, height, weight, and activity level. Boys usually need to eat more than girls, and active people need to eat more than less active people. Sometimes kids and teens feel hungrier than usual, because they're going through a growth spurt or changes to their bodies due to puberty.

Experts recommend that people worry more about *what* they eat than *how much* they eat. Still, it is a good idea to understand **portion sizes.** Here are some simple portion guidelines to keep in mind:

★ *A portion of meat is 3 ounces:* that's about the size of a deck of playing cards or a bar of soap.

★ *A portion of fruit or vegetables is one cup:* that's about the size of your closed fist. (It's also the size of a medium apple.)

★ *A portion of pasta is one cup:* measure it out before you cook it.

★ *A portion of ice cream is one-half cup:* that's about the size of a tennis ball.

These guidelines may seem simple enough, but a funny thing happens when we go to restaurants. Portion sizes can seem all out-of-whack. That's because most restaurants in North America serve portions two or three times bigger than what people should be eating. Holy macaroni! Do your best to stick to these guidelines when you eat out.

You're Not Eating *that,* Are You?

Most people like to eat a less-than-healthy snack between meals now and then. You know, snacks like chips, soft drinks, candy bars, or cupcakes. And many of us will eat a not-exactly-super-good-for-you meal once in a while, too. This might be a fast-food burger and fries or a couple slices of greasy pizza.

You might expect to read that you should **never, ever, not in a million years** eat these foods. But guess what? Those foods are okay sometimes. Everyone deserves a treat now and then. Treating yourself to something special is part of taking care of yourself. But the key word here is . . . you guessed it . . . **sometimes.** Foods like this are best left for once-in-a-while, something-special-type treats.

Here's why: they fill you up, but they aren't balanced for good health. They provide more fat, sugar, or salt than important nutrients. And when we say they "fill you up," we mean they can *really* fill you up.

So what's wrong with being full? Read on.

Full of What?

Energy is measured in **calories.** Almost every bite of food has a certain number of calories, and everything you do uses up a certain number of calories. Boys between the ages of 9 and 13 may need to eat anywhere from 1,800 to 2,600 calories a day, depending on how tall, heavy, and active they are. Girls of the same age usually need between 1,600 and 2,200 calories.

Imagine an 11-year-old boy whose body needs about 2,000 calories a day. Let's call him Lenny. And let's say one day Lenny eats:

1. a muffin from a bakery (about 560 calories) and an 8-ounce glass of 1% milk (about 100 calories) for breakfast

2. a fast-food burger (about 500 calories), large order of fries (about 500 calories), and 12-ounce soft drink (about 150 calories) for lunch

3. a 2-ounce chocolate bar (about 280 calories) for a snack

Add it all up, and Lenny has put away about 2,110 calories already, and it's not even close to dinnertime yet! When you eat more calories than your body can use, the extra get stored as fat. And that's not good for your health.

In 2007 in the United States, $1 out of every $10 spent on food was spent on fast food.

But the most important thing about that diet is not the number of calories. It's the lack of nutrients it provides. Those foods don't have nearly enough vitamins, minerals, calcium, fiber, or other important nutrition that your body needs. This can leave a guy like Lenny feeling tired, unfocused, and not quite his usual happy self. Those foods not only don't help you, but they fill you up so that you're not hungry for foods that *do* help you.

It's double trouble.

Now, let's imagine Lenny ate this instead:

1. Bowl of cereal with 1% milk (about 210 calories) and a cup of sliced strawberries (about 80 calories) for breakfast

2. Ham, cheese, and spinach sandwich on whole wheat bread (about 350 calories), an apple (about 80 calories), an 8-ounce cup of 1% milk (about 100 calories), and a cup of fruit yogurt (about 110 calories) for lunch

3. A 2-ounce chocolate candy bar (about 280 calories) for a snack

This diet provides lots of nutrients to help Lenny feel and look his best. Plus, it's only about 1,210 calories. Even though Lenny treated himself to a candy bar after school, he can still eat a healthy snack and dinner without getting too many calories.

What Do Vitamins and Minerals Do, Anyway?

Vitamins and minerals help your body in many different ways. That's why it's so important to eat a variety of foods—so you get a variety of these nutrients. Here's an explanation of what some vitamins and minerals can do for you.

Vitamin	What It's Good For
A	Improves eyesight and sense of taste; helps cells grow
B2	Improves health of skin, nails, and hair; improves eyesight
C	Strengthens immune system; heals wounds; protects from viruses and bacteria; reduces cholesterol
D	Helps build strong bones and teeth; regulates mood and pain; improves immune system
E	Helps protect your cells from damage

Mineral	What It's Good For
Calcium	Super important for strong bones and teeth
Iron	Helps red blood cells carry oxygen to all parts of the body so you feel energized
Magnesium	Helps muscles and nerves work their best; helps create energy
Zinc	Helps you grow and develop; improves your immune system; heals wounds

Where to Get It

Carrots, yellow fruits, green leafy veggies, dairy products

Milk, liver, cheese, green leafy veggies, fish

Citrus fruits, kiwi fruit, berries, tomatoes, cauliflower, potatoes, green leafy veggies, peppers

Dairy products, green leafy veggies, sardines, salmon, tuna, exposure to sunlight; many people get too little vitamin D because they don't get enough sun, so they may need a supplement

Nuts, green leafy veggies, avocados, and whole grains

Where to Get It

Dairy products, green leafy veggies, broccoli, and soy foods

Red meat, pork, fish, poultry, lentils, beans, soy foods, green leafy veggies, and raisins; Some cereals and grain products are fortified with iron

Whole grains, nuts, seeds, green leafy veggies, potatoes, beans, avocados, bananas, kiwi, broccoli, shrimp, and chocolate (oh, yeah!)

Red meat, poultry, seafood, nuts, soy foods, dairy products, whole grains, and fortified breakfast cereals

What About Snacking?

Many not-so-healthy foods are particularly tempting at snack time—foods like chips, flavored crackers, cookies, candy bars, cakes, muffins, and soft drinks. And it's no wonder: those foods are tasty, and many are premade and packaged, so they're easy to grab. They seem perfect for snacking.

It *is* okay to treat yourself occasionally, but remember these foods don't help you. In fact, most of them are actually *bad* for you. Salty snacks like chips and French fries can have lots of fat in them. Candy and other sweets usually have WAY more sugar than your body needs. Eating too much sugar can lead to weight gain, tooth decay, and other health problems. Also, these foods are often processed and contain chemicals. Many contain trans fats, which contribute to serious diseases like heart disease.

Snacking can be a positive part of a healthy diet—if you focus on **smart snacking.** Keep healthy "grabbable" food around to help you do that.

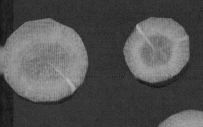

Here are some ideas:

- ★ dried fruit mix

- ★ pretzels—put them in a small cup or bowl

- ★ vegetables cut up, such as carrot or celery sticks, sliced cucumber, and red bell pepper wedges

- ★ lowfat yogurt or smoothie

- ★ water—instead of soda or sugar juices

- ★ fruits—apple slices, orange wedges, pears, grapes

- ★ trail mix

- ★ whole grain crackers and cheese or peanut butter

What if You're Overweight?

What if you are overweight or don't feel good about your body? If that sounds like you, talk to your school nurse, your doctor, or some other healthcare professional. He or she can help you create a healthy eating plan.

In the meantime, it's important that you do NOT "go on a diet." Remember, a real diet is simply what you eat. *Going* on a diet, or *dieting,* is usually unhealthy. Dieting means restricting what you eat and depriving yourself of things you want to eat. It means constantly weighing yourself and worrying about your weight. Dieting can be bad for your self-esteem—and usually for your body, too. Instead, make smarter decisions about what you eat, and make sure to get regular exercise.

Here are three things you can start doing right now that will lead to results:

★ *Drink water instead of soda.* Water has zero calories and makes you feel full so you eat less. Soft drinks are loaded with calories. They also have artificial chemicals and often caffeine, which are not good for kids. Even diet soft drinks have calories and chemicals.

★ *Eat fruit instead of drinking fruit juice.* Fruit has fewer calories and more fiber than juice (fiber helps with digestion and helps you feel full, so you don't overeat).

★ *Cut way back on high-calorie snacks like chips and cookies.*

Another thing you can do if you're struggling with your weight is to always remember the number one:

★ Eat all three daily meals—don't skip even *one.*

★ Eat at least *one* fruit and vegetable at every meal.

★ Eat *one* serving of the main course.

★ Eat *one* serving size of the main course.

★ Eat *one* item on a sandwich (peanut butter or jelly, ham or cheese).

★ Eat *one* serving of grains (whole wheat bread, for example) at a meal.

★ Eat *one* or two snacks daily.

★ Get at least *one*-half hour of activity daily (it doesn't have to be all at once).

★ If you need to make changes in your diet, make *one* change at a time.

Write It Down: A Small Step That Can Lead to Big Results

Do you know how much food you eat? Do you *really* know? Do you sometimes snack without really thinking about it? How much of the food you eat is junk food?

One easy but effective way to cut down on calories is to keep track of your diet. Most people underestimate how much they eat. Once you see what you're really eating, it's easier to make changes.

If you're trying to curb your appetite, it can help to brush your teeth. This changes the flavor in your mouth and gets your mind off eating.

For one week, record everything you eat or drink by jotting it into a notebook or keeping a file on your computer. This is called a "Food Diary." Be precise, and don't leave out anything! Count every snack, every drink, and every item at every meal. Also jot down a letter "E" for every day you get at least one half hour of exercise.

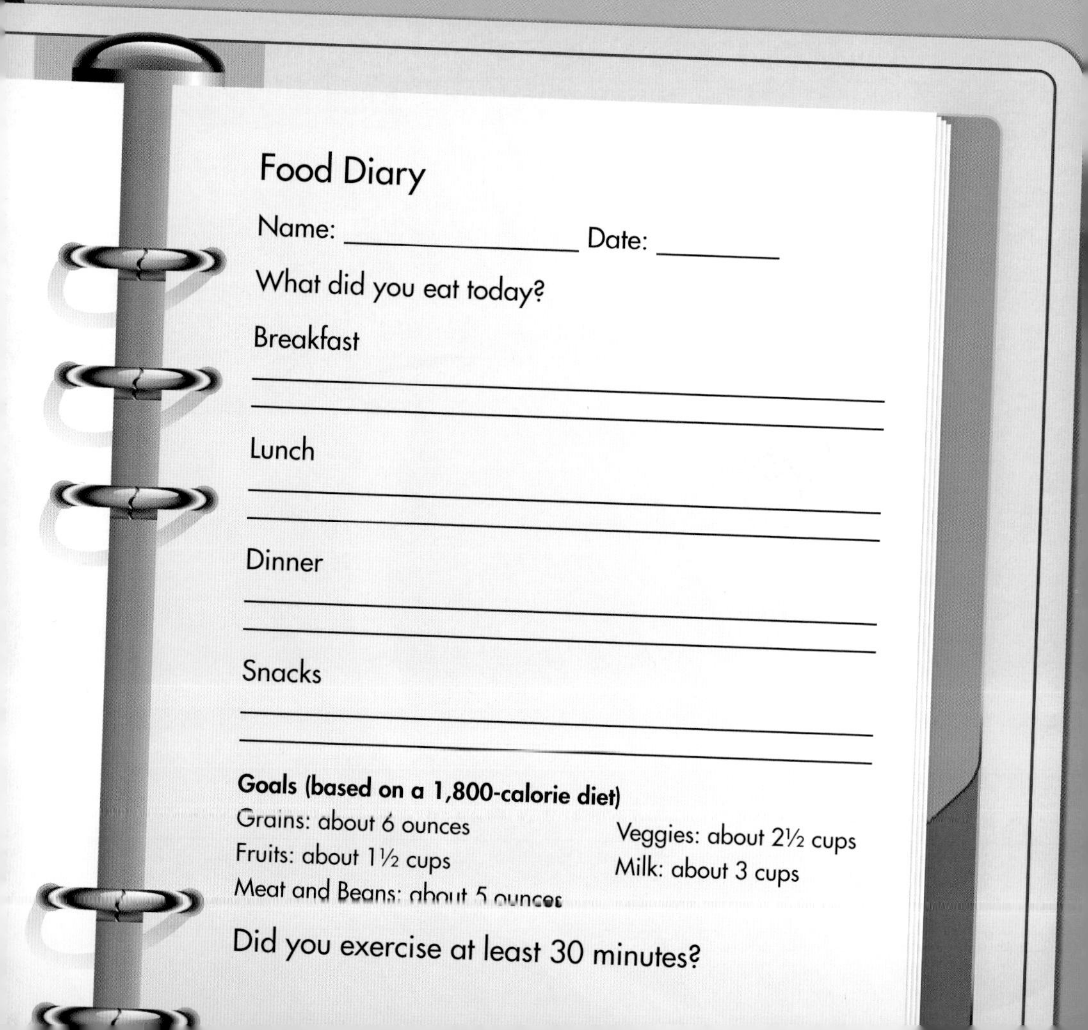

Food Diary

Name: _____ Date: _____

What did you eat today?

Breakfast
_____
_____

Lunch
_____
_____

Dinner
_____
_____

Snacks
_____
_____

Goals (based on a 1,800-calorie diet)

Grains: about 6 ounces

Fruits: about 1½ cups

Meat and Beans: about 5 ounces

Veggies: about 2½ cups

Milk: about 3 cups

Did you exercise at least 30 minutes?

After the week, look back at your notes. What do you see? Did you eat more than you expected? Are you exercising enough? Do you see areas where you could easily make improvements?

Studies show that every cell in your body reacts to your thoughts—so think positive thoughts! **Be grateful for every positive step you take.** If you usually drink two cans of soda a day, and you cut that down to one, that's a positive step! Imagine yourself craving healthy foods. Picture yourself being active. When you do these things, you program your brain to follow through.

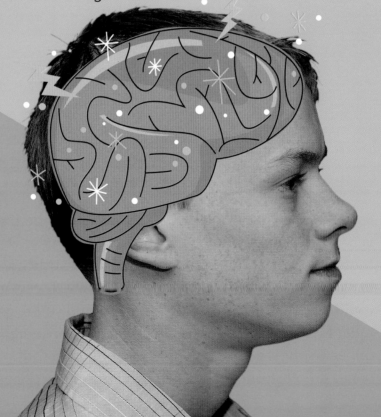

What if You're Underweight?

Some kids and teens have trouble *gaining* weight. If you're very skinny compared to your friends, or if you're worried that you might be underweight, talk to a healthcare expert. You may simply have a slender body type. Or you could be going through a growth spurt and you're growing taller faster than your body can fill in. But for some, being underweight is a real problem. It could mean that your bones aren't strong enough and you may get sick easily.

If you need to gain weight, it's important you do it in a healthy way. Here are some suggestions:

★ Eat smaller, more frequent meals to keep your energy level even throughout the day

★ Eat healthy snacks with lots of calories, like peanut butter, cheese, avocado, and meat

★ Drink 30 minutes before or after you eat, so you don't fill up on liquids at mealtime

★ If you have trouble remembering to eat, post reminders for yourself—perhaps on your calendar, notebook, or in your locker

★ Ask a parent to keep foods you like around the house

★ Even though exercise burns calories, don't stop doing it— it's important to keep your bones and muscles strong

A food diary can help with trying to eat more just like it can with trying to eat less. See page 62 for more about food diaries.

When Eating Becomes an Illness: Eating Disorders

Sometimes, the way people eat or think about eating can make them really sick. They may eat way too little or way too much. This is called an eating disorder. Eating disorders can lead to serious medical problems or even death. The most common eating disorders include:

★ *Anorexia nervosa.* This is when a person does not eat enough food for fear of gaining weight. They may exercise too much, too. People with anorexia think they are too fat no matter how thin they are.

★ *Bulimia nervosa.* Bulimia is when someone eats huge quantities of food in a short amount of time and then vomits or takes laxatives (pills to make you go to the bathroom) to get rid of the food. Again, this is done out of fear of gaining weight.

★ *Binge eating.* People with this disorder eat large amounts of food at one time and can't seem to help themselves. They may be eating to cope with an emotion such as stress, sadness, or fear, though they may not know it. Binge eating is also known as compulsive eating.

Here are common signs that a person has an eating disorder:

★ Dieting even when not overweight

★ Eating in secret

★ Thinking or talking about food all the time

★ Restricting foods or food groups

★ Cutting foods into overly small bites or pushing food around the plate without eating it

★ Physical changes, such as weight loss, weakness, headaches, and dizziness

★ Withdrawing from friends and family

★ Feeling like you have to exercise constantly

★ Having a fear of food or eating

★ Doing poorly in school with these other signs

★ Vomiting after eating meals, or using laxatives

★ Eating huge portions of food at one time

★ Wearing baggy clothes to hide thinness

★ Feeling cold all the time

If you are concerned that you or one of your friends has an eating disorder, talk to a parent or a healthcare professional such as a school nurse right away. You can call the National Association of Anorexia Nervosa and Associated Disorders to get free hotline counseling. You can call Monday through Friday, 9 a.m. to 5 p.m. Central time. They can help you find support groups and healthcare professionals who can help you. You can also learn more about eating disorders and how to prevent them. Their phone number is (857) 831-3438. Check out their Web site for more information (www.anad.org). Another good place to learn more about eating and eating disorders is the KidsHealth Web site (kidshealth.org).

Make a Plan and Stick with It

Have you ever looked in the refrigerator or cupboard and found nothing to eat? The fridge may be full of food, but nothing looks good. This may be because you don't know what you're looking for or you are not really hungry. Often, we eat when we're bored or we do it without really thinking. Other times, when we think we're hungry, we're really just thirsty. Still other times, we may be tempted by unhealthy foods like soda, candy, and chips whether we're hungry or not.

Emotional Eating

People eat for many reasons, not just hunger. Have you ever eaten . . .

- to feel better when you were stressed, sad, angry, lonely, or frustrated?
- because you were bored—for example, while watching TV?
- to celebrate something like a birthday or holiday?

When we eat for these reasons, we often "feed" our emotions with foods high in sugar or salt, such as cookies, ice cream, or chips. These foods may give us comfort. If you remember to think about *why* you are eating—and eat when you're hungry—you'll make better food decisions. Doing Get in Sync (pages 18–19) can help, too.

To give yourself the best chance of eating healthy, plan out your diet—and stick to your plan! You will probably need to include a family adult in all these steps to help you with the planning, shopping, and cooking.

1. Plan a healthy menu for every meal of the week— breakfast, lunch, and dinner every day, plus snacks. Remember to include lots of natural, colorful foods, including at least one fruit and vegetable with every meal. (See pages 35–36.)

2. Make a shopping list of all the food you'll need to prepare the meals.

3. Go to the grocery store and help choose the food.

4. Prepare the meals as you have planned them. Try not to make any changes.

Here's what we mean about not making changes. Say you planned to have a turkey sandwich, an orange, carrot sticks, and a carton of milk for lunch. Then your friend sits next to you in the lunchroom. He has an extra can of soda and asks if you want it. *Don't slip from your plan and drink that soft drink!* It may sound really good— and hey, it's free, which is even better—but saying no will help you stick to your plan. And it's the healthy choice.

Great Recipes Kids Can Make
In addition to MyPyramid.gov, lots of sources offer tasty, healthy, easy-to-make recipes for young people. Try:

- **KidsHealth.** Go to www.kidshealth.org, click the "teens" tab, then click "recipes."

- **Dole SuperKids.** Go to dole5aday.com and click on "kids cookbook" for recipes from pizza to parfaits.

- *The Everything Kids' Cookbook* by Sandra K. Nissenberg. The author is a registered dietician (a food and nutrition expert) and her book includes 90 recipes kids can make.

- *Children's of Minnesota—Integrative Medicine.* Go to childrensintegrativemed.org and click on "chowkids" for healthy recipes that taste good.

When you're at home, eat together as a family as often as possible. Make that part of your plan, too. Turn off the TV, phones, and games, and encourage family members to have fun. Try not to talk about problems. Make mealtime a pleasant time. Family meals are more likely to be nutritious than meals grabbed on the run or eaten alone or in front of the TV. And eating together gives your family a chance for some together time.

Sometimes it may be hard to stick to your plan. Sometimes you really crave something salty or fatty, and sometimes you overeat. When you struggle with your healthy diet, try one or more of the following B³ skills. They'll help your body, mind, and spirit, and they can give you the strength you need to stick with it—even when you don't feel like it.

B³ Skill:
Mindful Eating

No matter what your weight or how healthy your diet is, you can improve your eating habits and make eating more enjoyable using **mindful eating.**

Mindfulness means giving full attention to what you are doing, thinking, and feeling. Mindful *eating* means paying attention to the taste, texture (feeling), smell, and look of the food you eat. It also means paying attention to *where* you eat, *why* you eat, and *how much* you eat.

The benefits of eating mindfully include:

★ You will eat more slowly, so your body will feel full before you eat too much.

★ You will digest your food more easily and completely.

★ You will have a chance to appreciate the flavor, texture, and taste of the food you are eating, so you really enjoy it.

★ You have time to think about how you are connected to the earth and your food sources.

★ You have time to be grateful for all that you have.

★ You may feel calmer.

Mindful eating actually starts before you begin eating.

Here's how you do it:

★ **Pay attention to how your body feels.** Eat when you feel hungry.

★ **Pay attention to your feelings.** Are you eating because you want to feel better about something? Are you bored, frustrated, worried, or stressed?

★ **Pay attention to how you feel about the food.** Do you think the food you're going to eat is "good for you"? Do you think it's "bad"?

★ **Pay attention to the food you eat.** Look closely at it. Notice the texture, the smell, and the temperature. Think about these details.

Now take a bite. Start with something small, like a grape or a small bite of something. Put it in your mouth and feel it there. Is it smooth, crunchy, juicy, hard, or soft? Chew slowly. Listen to the sound it makes in your mouth. Notice the flavor and how it changes as you chew. Notice how it makes you feel when you eat something you enjoy very slowly. Does it make you smile?

B³ skill:
The Nose Knows

Have you ever smelled a fragrant flower and noticed that you exhaled more slowly and you felt a smile on your face? Have you ever walked into the kitchen after a bad day and noticed that you felt better once you smelled dinner cooking? Or have you noticed that you feel comforted when you smell the familiar scent of a parent or your bed?

The changes you felt are real—you didn't imagine them! Smelling good smells can help you feel better in many ways, including feeling more relaxed and comfortable. Using smells to help you feel better is called aromatherapy. The nerve from your nose has a connection to deep areas of your brain. That connection has a powerful effect on how your body feels. In aromatherapy, you use oils that come from plants like lavender, peppermint, and rosemary, and also from fruits like orange, lime, and lemon. Aromatherapy can even help control your appetite. Smells can tell your brain that you are full.

It's helpful to smell your favorite oil at the same time you are doing a relaxation exercise such as Belly Breathing or Imagine That! (see page 96). They work well together to get your body even more relaxed than either one can do alone.

You will need high-quality oils, called "essential oils." You can find them at health food stores, natural food co-ops, at some drug stores, and on the Internet. Buy medical type oils so you know they are of good quality. Look for oils that say "organic" on them. That means they're all natural and not made from chemicals.

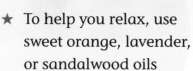

★ To help you relax, use sweet orange, lavender, or sandalwood oils

★ To help control your appetite, use Scotch pine or grapefruit oils

Important: To be safe, get a parent or other adult to help you buy aromatherapy oils and do the activity.

★ To ease an upset stomach, use ginger or spearmint oils

★ To help digestion, use peppermint or lemon oils

★ To get extra energy, use lime, Scotch pine, or grapefruit oils

★ To reduce stress, use lavender, frankincense, or chamomile oils

Here's how you do it:

Unscrew the cap from the bottle, hold it about one inch from your nostrils, and inhale slowly and deeply. Repeat once or twice. Each time you inhale, imagine the comforting scent traveling into your brain and sending out comforting messages to your body.

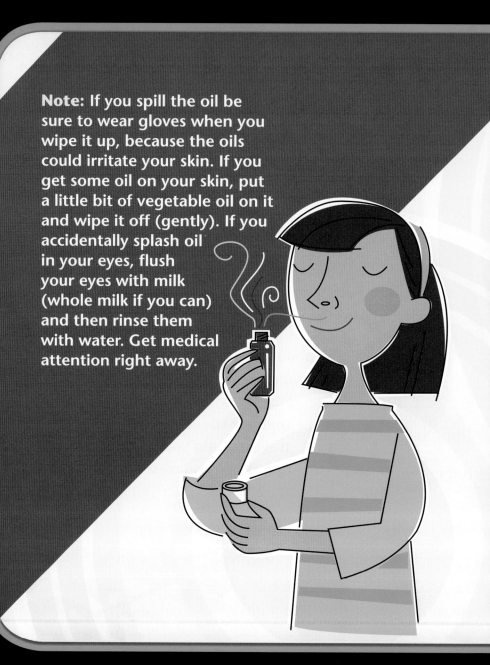

Note: If you spill the oil be sure to wear gloves when you wipe it up, because the oils could irritate your skin. If you get some oil on your skin, put a little bit of vegetable oil on it and wipe it off (gently). If you accidentally splash oil in your eyes, flush your eyes with milk (whole milk if you can) and then rinse them with water. Get medical attention right away.

B³ skill: Press to feel Better

Acupressure was developed in Asia about 5,000 years ago. It means applying pressure to specific spots on your body that can help you feel better. For example, if you feel like throwing up, a very powerful point on your wrist (see diagram on page 84) can make you feel better just by pushing on it! You have more than 300 of these spots all over your body for treating all kinds of symptoms. You can push on your acupressure points any time you want to feel more relaxed, ease pain or tension, gain energy, or even control your appetite.

Traditional Asian culture describes a life force, or "Qi" (pronounced "chee"), that flows through each person on special pathways. When these pathways become blocked, acupressure can unblock them so your Qi flows freely, making you more energized and healthy feeling.

Each acupressure point is connected by your nervous system to a place in your brain. Each place controls a particular symptom or feeling (like stomachaches or hunger). Pressing on the right acupressure point helps the body release chemicals that relieve the symptom or change the feeling. It also reduces tension and stress, relaxes muscles, and allows better blood flow. That brings more oxygen and nutrients to the area. Not only that, it strengthens your immune system, too!

You can stimulate these special acupressure points using one of the following:

★ your finger

★ a pencil eraser

★ acupressure beads

★ a wooden acupressure tool →

Here's how you do it:

Look at the acupressure points diagrams on pages 84–85 and select a point you want to stimulate. A good place to start is a point called the Sea of Tranquility. It is located on the center of your breastbone and helps release anxiety and negative emotions.

Once you've selected a point, push on it using your finger or whatever tool you've selected for 30 seconds to one minute. Use medium pressure, making small circles. If you use your finger, you may begin to feel your pulse. That's a good sign, because it means your circulation is increasing in this area. Repeat this several times, every 15 minutes, and take a few Belly Breaths after each time.

Sea of Tranquility
On the center of your breastbone, this point helps release anxiety and negative emotions.

Sea of Energy
This point, located three finger widths below your belly button, can refresh you when your body feels weak or overly tired.

Attention Grown-Ups
If you are pregnant, talk to your doctor before doing acupressure. Some acupressure points can cause early labor.

Inner Gate
Located in the middle of the inside of your wrist, two and one-half finger widths above your wrist crease, this point relieves anxiety, stomachaches, and the feeling you have to throw up.

Ear Hunger Point
The bump in front of your ear opening can be pressed or squeezed to help control the urge to overeat.

Three Mile Point
Found just on the outside of your shinbone four finger widths below your knee cap, this point can improve digestion and circulation; relieve anxiety, headaches, and fatigue; and boost the immune system.

Get your Imagine That! skill involved, too. As you press on one of your points, imagine your finger or acupressure tool is sending healing energy into that spot.

Large Esteem
Located on the back inside corner of the nail bed of your big toe, this point helps you feel more assertive and improves self-esteem.

MOVIN' AND IMPROVIN'

Exercise Is Excellent

What do you think of when you hear the word **"exercise"**? Maybe you think of sit-ups, push-ups, and jumping jacks. Maybe the idea of that kind of exercise makes you want to jumping-jack right out the door and escape. But hold on—don't bail out just yet. Exercise doesn't have to be a chore. It can be healthy *and* enjoyable.

Word Watch

Stress: strain, worry, or pressure

Anxiety: strong worry or fear

Depression: an illness in which a person feels very sad or crabby most of the time

What's Good About Exercise

Exercise is an amazing medicine for your body, mind, and spirit. It can heal and strengthen all three. What is exercise good for? Here's just a short list of benefits.

EXERCISE . . .

* builds stronger bones and joints
* builds stronger muscles
* boosts your immune system (to fight off illness)
* gets more oxygen to your brain to help you think better
* gives you better concentration in school
* leads to greater flexibility
* increases your energy
* relieves stress, anxiety, and depression
* strengthens your heart and lungs, making them healthier
* helps you sleep better
* promotes positive feelings like joy
* gets you together with kids who like to do what you like

Word Watch
High blood pressure: when blood flow puts too much pressure on artery walls, which can lead to heart problems

But wait—there's more!
Exercise also stimulates endorphins that help you feel more relaxed and be in a better mood. It can help prevent the buildup of plaque in your arteries so blood can flow more smoothly, which helps prevent high blood pressure and heart disease.

And you know what? Exercise can be fun—do it with friends or make it a family event.

How Much Exercise Do You Need?

Humans use about 60 percent of the calories they consume each day for basic bodily functions, such as breathing, digesting, and pumping blood. You don't even have to think about it. The other 40 percent of your daily calories is burned off through activity. A lot of that you don't have to think about, either. That's because just about everything you do burns calories. That includes activities like brushing your teeth, taking a shower, getting dressed, setting the table, feeding the cat, laughing, and scratching an itch. Even watching TV and playing video games use energy, although those two "activities" burn about as many calories as sleeping (about one calorie per minute).

On top of all those regular things you do, your body needs at least 30 minutes of vigorous exercise every day. *Vigorous* means lively and energetic, but it doesn't all have to be done at one time. You can do 10 minutes here and 15 minutes there, or 20 minutes now and 20 later. Whatever it takes! Vigorous exercise helps you keep your body running like the high-performance machine it is.

Remember, though, that the activity should be *in addition* to your usual daily activities. So even though brushing your teeth and teasing your sister—you know, that stuff you do anyway—burn calories, those activities don't count as *vigorous* activity. You need actual exercise.

What Kind of Exercise?

Whatever kind gets you moving!

Remember, exercise can be fun. It *should* be fun. Give one or two of these activities a try:

★ riding your bike

★ dancing

★ jumping rope

★ running or playing tag

★ playing volleyball

★ playing touch football

★ playing soccer

★ playing active Wii games, like Wii Fit

★ skating

★ skateboarding

★ taking a walk, including walking the dog

★ golfing (carry your clubs—no cart)

★ swimming

★ bowling

★ playing hacky sack

★ playing catch (frisbee, baseball, football, water balloons, wadded up tin foil, etc.)

Exercise Is for Everyone

Everyone needs it, everyone can do it. You don't have to wear special clothes or sweatbands. You don't need weights or special equipment. And you don't have to go to a gym. You don't even have to call it "exercise." All you have to do is get moving.

Belly Breathing for Exercise

Taking a few Belly Breaths before, during, and after exercise is a great way to stay focused and feel the positive energy in your body, mind, and spirit. See pages 16–17.

You can do it as part of your regular day:

★ rake leaves or mow the lawn

★ sweep the floor

★ climb the stairs two at a time—then go down and do it again

★ clean your room

★ walk around while on the phone

★ walk or ride your bike when you go somewhere, like school, instead of getting a car ride

★ if you do get a ride, have the driver drop you off a couple blocks away from your destination

★ take the long way when walking or biking somewhere

★ use the stairs instead of the elevator or escalator

★ lift food cans or jars (use them like weights)

★ take out the garbage

★ play with your siblings

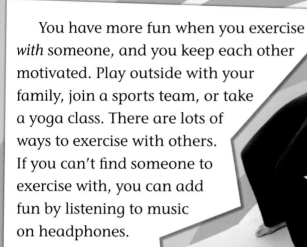

You have more fun when you exercise *with* someone, and you keep each other motivated. Play outside with your family, join a sports team, or take a yoga class. There are lots of ways to exercise with others. If you can't find someone to exercise with, you can add fun by listening to music on headphones.

Count Your Steps

Have you ever counted how many steps you take from your bedroom to the kitchen? Ever wondered how many steps you take in a day at school? How about during a walk around the block? You can keep track of your steps using a pedometer.

A pedometer is a tool that counts the steps you take while you wear it. You can get one in the sports section of many stores or at a health club. They cost anywhere from $4 to $20. People who keep track of their steps tend to walk more than those who don't, so it's not just a way to be more aware of your exercise—it's a way to do more of it!

The Nose Knows Energy

If you need a boost before or during exercise, take a few deep breaths of peppermint or lemon oil. It will boost your energy. See pages 77–80 for more about aromatherapy.

B³ skill:
Imagine That!

It might seem hard to believe, but changing what you're thinking about can completely change the way you feel. Creating pleasant, positive, healthy images in your mind can help you make good food choices and succeed in increasing your activity. Use Imagine That! whenever your self-esteem needs a boost, you are struggling with making good eating choices, or you need extra motivation to exercise. Or, make this skill a part of your daily routine to help keep your body, mind, and spirit balanced all the time.

Find a quiet, comfortable place to sit or lie down. This skill works better the more active your brain is, so give your brain lots of details. Imagine lots of colors, shapes, and objects. Hear pleasant sounds and smell smells that please you. Notice what you can touch or what touches you. Make it all comforting and relaxing.

Here's how you do it:

Get in the right frame of mind by imagining you are somewhere that is fun, safe, and pleasant for you. This might be your room, the beach, a grandparent's home, a ball field, or somewhere else. Imagine you are doing something you really enjoy, like playing a sport, reading a book, or playing with a dog or cat. Remember to imagine lots of details—the smell of the dog's fur, the feel of the book in your hands, the warmth of the sand between your toes, the sound of water lapping on the shore. As you do this, notice how your body feels.

Now picture yourself just the way you would like to be—strong, healthy, and physically fit. Imagine yourself eating healthy food and how it makes the inside of your body work just right! Imagine being active and how it makes your body feel great. Imagine that you can see yourself in a mirror. See all the positive parts of yourself.

Now imagine seeing yourself a little bit older than you are right now. You are physically fit, and you are the boss of your body, mind, and spirit. You are proud of your success.

B³ Skill: Yoga

Yoga is a practice that focuses on connecting your body, mind, and spirit. By combining breathing exercises, physical poses, and meditation, you can improve your strength, flexibility, and balance. It helps you develop better body awareness, coordination, and overall health. And it burns calories, conditions your heart, and lowers your blood pressure. Yoga can also help relieve depression and anger, reduce anxiety, calm your mind, and improve your mood. This makes you feel better about yourself.

Some yoga poses are designed to calm and focus the mind and body. Others can energize them. Doing yoga regularly can also help you learn to relax and think more clearly. In other words, yoga can make you feel *good!*

The word *yoga* has several meanings, which all refer to a balancing of your thoughts and feelings. One meaning for the word is "unity." Another is "stillness." Scientific studies done in the United States and India show that a program that includes yoga poses, eating changes, and breathing exercises can help with weight loss. Yoga is also known to help with physical problems such as headaches, stomachaches, anxiety, sleep problems, and back problems. Because it helps calm the mind, you may feel more confident and think more clearly.

Do yoga on a nonslip surface with bare feet. Using a yoga mat is a good idea so you have your own space and keeps your hands and feet from slipping. If you've never done yoga before, start slowly.

The earliest evidence of yoga are stone slabs of people in yoga poses. They were found in India and were dated at 3000 BC.

You can do yoga by yourself, following the instructions in this book. But it is important that you stick to these basic poses and do only what your body is comfortable and strong enough to do. Listen to your body! If something hurts or doesn't feel comfortable, stop doing it.

The best way to learn yoga is from a certified yoga teacher who can show you how to do the poses safely and get the most out of them. Most yoga poses can be modified or broken down to make them accessible to anyone—even someone in a wheelchair or hospital bed. A teacher will also teach you about breathing, relaxing, and how yoga can help you think more clearly and positively.

Tree pose

This pose helps the

★ **Body** by increasing your balance and strength

★ **Mind** by increasing your focus, improving your mental balance, and helping you be more thoughtful

★ **Spirit** by giving you a feeling of peacefulness

It is important to always recognize your own strength and limitations. If a pose feels wrong or painful, do not do it.

Here's how you do it:

Stand up straight. Put your weight on your right leg and stay until you feel balanced. (It's okay to lightly touch a wall or table to help steady you.) Now bend your left leg and put your foot on your right leg—wherever it rests comfortably above or below your knee, but *not* on your knee.

Breathe.

Bring your hands together in front of your chest or above your head. Breathe deeply and calmly while you balance.

To release, slowly lower your arms and bring your weight back to both feet.

Next, repeat the pose balancing on your left leg.

Warrior II pose

This classic yoga pose helps the

★ **Body** by giving you strength

★ **Mind** by helping you think positively and giving you confidence

★ **Spirit** by giving you determination, perseverance, and bravery

Here's how you do it:
Stand tall. Step your feet apart to a comfortable distance (about one leg length apart). Turn your right foot out to the side (90 degrees).

Now bend your right knee, keep your knee in line with (or directly above) your heel. Keep your left leg straight, pushing down through the left heel.

Raise your arms and hold them steady at shoulder height. Imagine one straight line from the fingertip of your right hand to the fingertip of your left hand. Turn your head to the right. Feel the strength in your legs, back, and shoulders.

Breathe.

To release, turn your head to the front, lower your arms, and straighten your right leg.

Next, repeat the pose on the other side.

Child's pose

This pose helps the

★ **Body** by aiding digestion

★ **Mind** by helping you focus

★ **Spirit** by calming you and reducing anxiety

Here's how you do it:

Sit on your knees. Let your arms hang by your sides.

Breathe in.

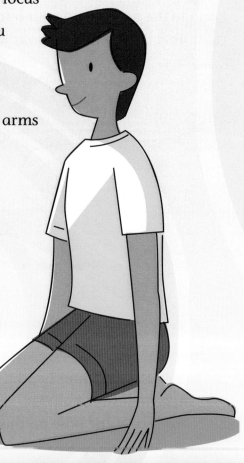

Breathe out. While breathing out, fold forward, lowering your head and back toward your knees. Your knees can be together or spread wide apart. Let your arms rest by your sides or spread out in front of you.

Breathe.
To release, slowly roll up your spine until you are sitting on your knees.

Be the Boss of Your Lifestyle

Eating and exercise are part of your lifestyle—things you do every day that have a big influence on how you feel and how happy you are. Other important parts of your lifestyle are:

★ **Sleep:** Most kids and teens need 9 to 10 hours of quality sleep each night to refresh their body, mind, and spirit. B³ skills such as Belly Breathing, Imagine That!, and Aromatherapy can help you relax and feel positive emotions when you go to sleep.

★ **Life management:** Give yourself a break by not committing to too many activities. Even if all the things you're doing are fun, you can wear yourself out if you don't have enough downtime. Remember, too, that you don't have to be perfect or the best at everything you do. Do your best, but remember that nobody is perfect.

★ **Social supports:** Do activities with family or friends— hang out and have fun together. Play! Have a good laugh with family and friends every day: tell jokes, watch a silly movie or TV show, check out a funny Web site, or put on a goofy play together. And remember to make mealtime a family activity whenever possible. Eat together and enjoy each other's company.

Remember, your body is amazing—and so are your mind and spirit. By taking control of your self-esteem and your food and fitness, you are tapping into the great power you have to be the boss of your body and live healthier. With a positive attitude and a commitment to your health, you have everything you need to

be fit

be strong

and be you!

NOTE TO GROWN-UPS

The Be the Boss of Your Body series is about kids taking charge of their own health, but that doesn't mean they don't need help from adults. This is especially true with diet and fitness. Parents and other caring adults are essential in helping children develop good eating habits and be physically fit. Eating well is a family affair. Young children are dependent on the food you offer them, and older children may adopt your eating habits. Whether the kids you're working with are overweight, underweight, or of normal weight, they need encouragement, positive reinforcement, love, and support while working to take control of their health.

Some of the most important things you can do to help are:

★ Read this book so you better understand what your child is doing.

★ Be available and supportive.

★ Listen to what your child tells you about how he or she feels, and try to understand.

★ Give your child as much control as possible to manage his or her diet and exercise.

★ Give praise and positive reinforcement for using the B³ skills; celebrate successes.

★ Encourage your child to continue participating in school and favorite activities.

★ Engage in self-care skills yourself.

Making Good Food and Fitness Decisions

The American Academy of Pediatrics (AAP) and the National Association of Nurse Practitioners have set guidelines and recommendations to help parents support their children in making good choices about eating and activity. Discuss nutrition with your child's healthcare provider, and start monitoring children's food and fitness when they are quite young. If you suspect your child has an eating disorder, contact your family doctor or another healthcare professional. For general pediatric health information, check out the AAP's Healthy Children Web site (www.healthychildren.org).

Recommendations for Eating

★ Model healthy eating with the foods you choose and the portions you eat and serve.

★ Teach children about appropriate portion sizes of all foods (see page 48).

★ Do not promote "diets."

★ Allow children to decide when they are full rather than insisting they clean their plates.

★ Offer a diet consisting of all nutrients and food groups (see pages 35–36).

★ Limit consumption of energy-dense (high calorie) food.

★ Limit the amount of sugar-sweetened beverages such as soda and juice.

★ Make sure kids get five or more servings of fruits and vegetables daily.

★ Eat a breakfast every day.

★ Limit meals outside of the home, especially at fast-food restaurants.

★ Regularly eat together as a family.

Recommendations for Shopping

★ Include children in planning meals, buying groceries, and making meals.

★ Make lists together of healthy snacks that are appealing.

★ Don't shop when you're hungry.

★ Leave junk food at the store. Keep healthy snacks on hand.

Recommendations for Physical Activity

★ Have a goal of 30–60 minutes of moderate to intense activity daily. *Remember that this time can be accumulated throughout the day rather than all at once.*

★ Promote physical activity at school and in childcare settings.

★ Be active with children. Allow them choices in deciding what to do. Go for a family walk once or twice a week.

★ Provide play equipment that increases physical activity.

Recommendations for Screen Time

★ Make time in front of TV, computer, and video game screens contingent on exercise: "If you play basketball for one hour, you can have screen time."

★ Limit screen time to two or fewer hours per day.

★ Don't allow TV viewing for children less than 2 years of age.

★ Do not put a TV in a child's bedroom.

Recommendations for
Supporting Children's Self-Esteem

★ Support their efforts to make healthy choices in eating and activity by praising successes and good choices, by providing resources they need, and by helping them when they need it.

★ Encourage and empathize. Don't criticize their eating, how they look, or their exercise.

★ Get professional help when you need it.

★ Get the entire family to participate in healthy eating.

Evidence suggests that people who engage in self-care activities live healthier, more productive lives. Teaching kids to look at their health from a holistic perspective—considering body, mind, and spirit—and teaching them self-care skills sets the stage for lifelong wellness and balance. By encouraging and helping your children with the skills in this book, and modeling the skills yourself, you can give them the confidence to uncover the wealth of talent and strength they possess and encourage them to actively participate in their health. These skills can make a positive difference in *your* life, too!

Please remember that this book is not intended as a replacement for professional medical or psychological consultation when they are needed. Children and adolescents who are having serious health problems or new onset of symptoms should be evaluated by their primary care provider. Problems that are acute, severe, and/or associated with other symptoms such as fever, nausea, or rash need to be evaluated and treated by a qualified healthcare professional.

INDEX

ABOUT THE AUTHORS

Rebecca Kajander, C.P.N.P., M.P.H., is a nurse practitioner who has treated children and adolescents for nearly 40 years. She has helped hundreds of children take care of themselves using self-care skills and has helped many more understand and live with ADHD. In 2000, Rebecca was named "Pediatric Nurse Practitioner of the Year" by the Minnesota chapter of the National Association of Pediatric Nurse Practitioners, and in 2009 she received a Distinguished Nurse Award from the University of Minnesota.

Rebecca has been a lifelong resident of Minnetonka, Minnesota. She's married and has a grown son. When not working, Rebecca enjoys yoga and doing just about anything outside.

Timothy Culbert, M.D., is a behavioral and developmental pediatrician with training in biofeedback, medical hypnosis, and holistic medicine. He gives presentations nationally and internationally and publishes widely on mind-body skills training with children and teens. He has helped kids in clinical practice for 17 years, with special interests in teaching kids self-care skills and complementary and alternative medicine.

Tim lives in Greenwood, Minnesota, with his wife, Heidi, and teenage children, Sam and Hannah. He enjoys traveling, cooking, writing, hiking, and various creative endeavors.

More Products from the

Be the Boss of Your BODY® Series

by Timothy Culbert, M.D., and Rebecca Kajander, C.P.N.P., M.P.H.

Everyone needs to see a doctor sometimes. But we all can do a lot to take care of our own health and wellness. These books and kits help kids and teens discover their body's natural healing abilities, explore how their body, mind, and spirit work together, learn simple self-care skills, and form better lifestyle habits—for now and a healthier future.

Books are available separately or as part of the kit.

Each book: Softcover; 64 pp.; color illust.; 8" x 8"

Each kit: Contains the book of your choice plus tools; 8¹/₁₆" x 8¹/₁₆" x 1½"; for ages 8 & up

Be the Boss of Your Pain Book
ISBN 978-1-57542-254-1

Kit with Pain Book
ISBN 978-1-57542-273-2

Be the Boss of Your Stress Book
ISBN 978-1-57542-256-5

Kit with Stress Book
ISBN 978-1-57542-275-6

Be the Boss of Your Sleep Book
ISBN 978-1-57542-255-8

Kit with Sleep Book
ISBN 978-1-57542-274-9

GET THESE TOOLS WITH THE BOOK OF YOUR CHOICE!

Caribiner   Acupressure Tool   Biofeedback Card   Stress Ball   Quick-Start Card   Pinwheel   Stickers

WARNING: CHOKING HAZARD—Small parts. Not for children under 3 yrs.

Other Great Books from Free Spirit

Free Spirit's Laugh & Learn™ Series
Solid information, a kid-centric point of view, and a sense of humor combine to make each book in our Laugh & Learn series an invaluable tool for getting through life's rough spots. For ages 8–13.

Each book: Softcover; 72–128 pp.; illust.; 5⅛" x 7"

See You Later, Procrastinator!

Dude, That's Rude!

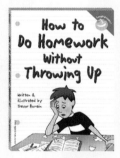

How to Do Homework Without Throwing Up

Bullies Are a Pain in the Brain

Stress Can Really Get on Your Nerves!

True or False? Tests Stink!

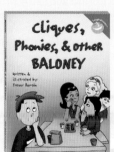

Get Organized Without Losing It

How to Take the GRRRR Out of Anger

Cliques, Phonies, & Other BALONEY

Siblings

Speak Up and Get Along!

by Scott Cooper

A handy toolbox of ways to get along with others, this book presents 21 strategies kids can learn and use to express themselves, build relationships, end arguments and fights, halt bullying, and beat unhappy feelings. Includes a note to adults. For ages 8–12.

Softcover; 128 pp.; 2-color; illust.; 6" x 9"

Stick Up for Yourself!

by Gershen Kaufman, Ph.D., Lev Raphael, Ph.D., and Pamela Espeland

Simple words and real-life examples teach assertiveness, responsibility, relationship skills, choice making, problem solving, goal setting, anger management, and more. For ages 8–12.

Softcover; 128 pp.; illust.; 6" x 9"

Good-Bye Bully Machine

by Debbie Fox and Allan L. Beane, Ph.D., illustrated by Debbie Fox

Kids learn what bullying is, why it hurts, and what they can do to end it. With its sophisticated collage art, lively layout, and straightforward text, *Good-Bye Bully Machine* engages kids and keeps them engaged. For ages 8 & up.

Softcover; 48 pp.; color illust.; 8" x 8" and Hardcover; 48 pp.; color illust.; 8¼" x 8¼"

What to Do When You're Scared & Worried

by James J. Crist, Ph.D.

From a dread of spiders to panic attacks, kids have worries and fears, just like adults. This is a book kids can turn to when they need advice, reassurance, and ideas. For ages 9–13.

Softcover; 128 pp.; 2-color; illust.; 5⅜" x 8⅜"

What to Do When You're Sad & Lonely

by James J. Crist, Ph.D.

All kids feel sad and lonely sometimes. Growing numbers of children are living with depression, a disease often mistaken for sadness. This reassuring book offers strategies and tips kids can use to beat the blues and blahs, get a handle on their feelings, make and keep friends, and enjoy their time alone. For ages 9–13.

Softcover; 128 pp.; 2-color; illust.; 5⅜" x 8⅜"

What to Do When Good Enough Isn't Good Enough

by Thomas S. Greenspon, Ph.D.

Most children don't know what perfectionism is, yet many are perfectionists or budding perfectionists. Nothing they do is good enough. This book helps kids understand what perfectionism is, how it hurts them, how to free themselves—and ultimately how to accept themselves as they are. For ages 9–13.

Softcover; 128 pp.; 2-color; illust.; 5⅜" x 8⅜"

For pricing information, to place an order, or to request a free catalog, contact.

Free Spirit Publishing Inc.
toll-free 800.735.7323 • help4kids@freespirit.com • www.freespirit.com